A mink, a fink, a Skating rink

What is a Noun?

noun: A word that names a person, animal, place or thing.

A mink, a fink, a Skating rink

What is a Noun?

by Brian P. Cleary
illustrated by Jenya Prosmitsky

BOOK HOUSE

Hill
is a
noun.

Mill
is a
noun.

Gown
is a
noun.

Crown is a noun.

In fact,
our whole
town is
a noun.

If it's a deck,
a duck,
or deer,

If it's
a crystal
chandelier,

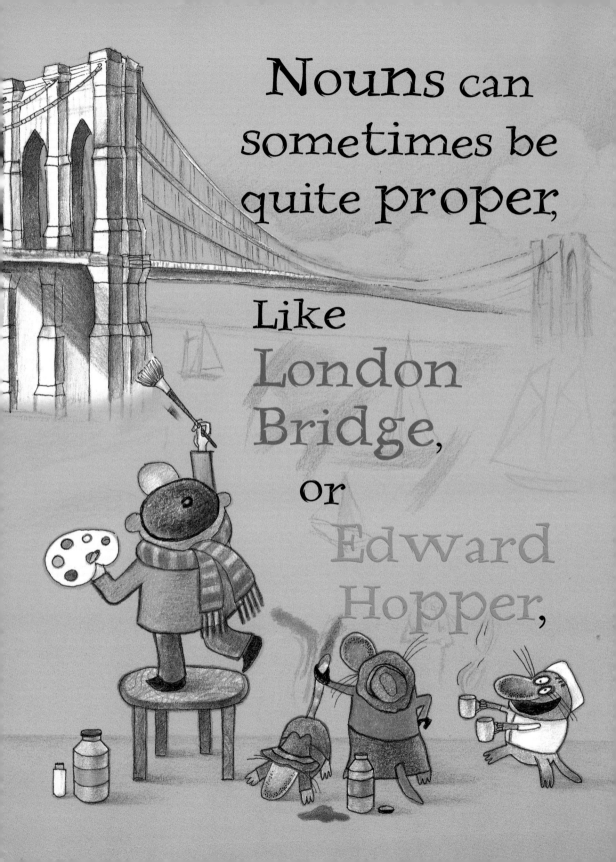

Nouns can sometimes be quite proper,

Like London Bridge, or Edward Hopper,

A jail,
a nail,
a bale
of hay,
The pool or park in
which you play,

A pound, a hound,
a pencil, or pear –

Nouns can be seen
everywhere.

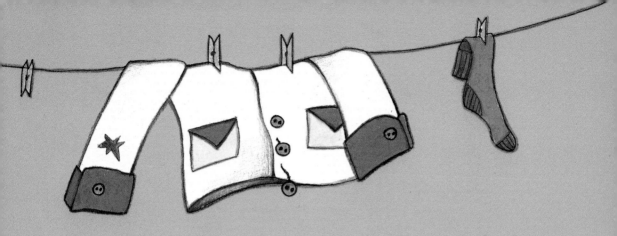

A pocket, button,
sleeve or cuff –

A noun can simply
be your stuff.

A mink,
a fink,
a skating rink,
A cake,
a rake,
your kitchen
sink,

The pope, some soap

that's on a rope,
A downtown shop,
a downhill slope.

A house,
a mouse,
a broken
clock,

New Mexico,
an old
white
sock,

WELCOME
TO
SANTA FE

Some tar,
a bar,
a baseball
star,
The place where
mother
parks
her car.

A noun
can be your
Auntie
Lynn,

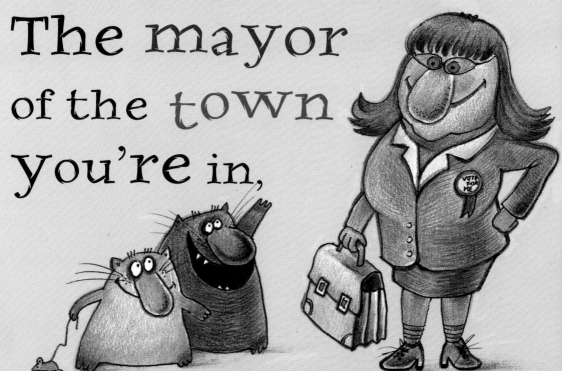

The mayor
of the town
You're in,

Your friend who tells you awful jokes –

A noun can be your favourite folks.

A collar,
a scholar,
a handful
of sand,

Saxes and
faxes, the brass
in the band,

A cat,
a bat,
your
grandma's
hat–

Nouns are a little
of this and that.

If it's a place of any kind –

A mountain, hall, or road number 9,

If it's a country, county, or town,

Then surely, Shirley, it's a noun.

And so is a poodle, cherry strudel,

a fork, a cork, a curly noodle,

A king,
a queen,
some
gasoline,

A red
raspberry
ice machine.

If it's a boat or coat or clown,

It's simple, Simon, it's a noun!

AUTHOR: BRIAN P. CLEARY is the author of several other books for children, including *To root, to toot, to parachute: What is a Verb?*

ILLUSTRATOR: JENYA PROSMITSKY grew up and studied art in Kishinev, Moldova, and now lives in Minneapolis in the USA. Her two cats, Henry and Freddy, were vital to her illustrations for this book.

To Molly, Matt, and Andy — three very proper nouns — B.P.C.

To my mum, who has always been crazy about cats, and my dad, who surprised me by bringing home a kitten when I was 10 — J.P.

Published in Great Britain in 2003 by
Book House, an imprint of
The Salariya Book Company Ltd
25 Marlborough Place, Brighton BN1 1UB

Please visit the Salariya Book Company at:
www.salariya.com
www.book-house.co.uk

ISBN 1 904194 63 X

A catalogue record for this book is available from the British Library.

Printed and bound in USA.